I0530744

the
Little Gold Book

Doughnut Books

About This Book

     The Little Gold Book was written by an anonymous group of heroin addicts in 2015. The Heroin Anonymous Literature Committee in Portland, Oregon included people of different backgrounds, lengths of sobriety, and reasons for participation. However, each committee member felt called to contribute. They shared the belief (from personal experience) that the Twelve Steps of Heroin Anonymous could save and change their lives.

     Certain phrases, words, and terms appear throughout *The Little Gold Book* which may sound familiar. Some of them come from other Twelve Step literature, and are cited when appropriate. No copyright infringement is intended. The manuscript is presented as it was written, in its most complete form. It is a representation and interpretation of the Twelve Steps, as lived by the members who contributed their time, energy, and heart to creating this book.

     The draft of *The Little Gold Book* was submitted for approval to the Heroin Anonymous World Services Board in 2015. However, the manuscript was never conference-approved. As such, this book should be considered an important perspective on the Twelve Steps of recovery, but not a replacement for the literature used by, and approved by, HA.

All profits from *The Little Gold Book* are donated to the Portland fellowship of Heroin Anonymous.

Doughnut Books
Portland, Oregon
doughnut-books.com

ISBN (paperback) 979-8-9991901-3-0

Cover design and interior formatting by FZ Boda
Written by the members of the Portland, Oregon
Heroin Anonymous Literature Committee, 2015

The Twelve Steps

1. We admitted we were powerless over heroin—that our lives had become unmanageable.

2. Came to believe that a Power greater than ourselves could restore us to sanity.

3. Made a decision to turn our will and our lives over to the care of God as we understood Him.

4. Made a searching and fearless moral inventory of ourselves.

5. Admitted to God, to ourselves, and to another human being the exact nature of our wrongs.

6. Were entirely ready to have God remove all these defects of character.

7. Humbly asked Him to remove our shortcomings.

8. Made a list of all persons we had harmed, and became willing to make amends to them all.

9. Made direct amends to such people wherever possible, except when to do so would injure them or others.

10. Continued to take personal inventory and when we were wrong promptly admitted it.

11. Sought through prayer and meditation to improve our conscious contact with God as we understood Him, praying only for knowledge of His will for us and the power to carry that out.

12. Having had a spiritual awakening as the result of these steps, we tried to carry this message to heroin addicts, and to practice these principles in all our affairs.

Getting Help

If you need help living, coping with trauma or harm, or staying sober, these resources offer support at no cost. Please reach out.

Heroin Anonymous

heroinanonymous.org

Suicide and Crisis Lifeline

988

The Rape, Abuse & Incest National Network (RAINN)

1-800-656-HOPE

The Trevor Project

1-866-488-7386

Adult Survivors of Child Abuse (ASCA)

info@ascasupport.org

415-937-1854

Table of Contents

Table of Contents

Who Are We?

Most of us couldn't answer that question honestly when we were in the grips of heroin addiction. We are people, from all walks of life, who have one thing in common: once we started using heroin, we found it was impossible to stop. We found that the drug that was once so comforting removed any trace of comfort from our lives. Eventually, we came to see what heroin had done to us—how it had destroyed the most important things in our lives. Still, we could not stop using. We were sick with heroin and we were sick without it. The world we lived in became dark and bleak. All sense of hope was lost, and any thought of reform was broken. We resigned ourselves to a life of pain and suffering.

Many of us would describe ourselves

somewhere on the spectrum between "scum of the earth" and "self-sacrificing saviors of the world." The truth was, we no longer knew. We couldn't imagine life without heroin in one form or another. The worse things got, the more we clung to the one thing that made us feel comforted, safe, in control, and numb.

At first, we waded in the shallow waters of addiction, experimenting with different substances, combinations of chemicals, and a menagerie of prescription pills. Eventually, heroin crossed our path. Whether we first tried it was a pill or a powder, we noticed that we had an atypical response. Maybe we got busy while our friends nodded off. Maybe we dreamed fantastic dreams. Maybe we were full of strength and passion, inspired by the amazing force we felt inside. It was love at first high. But after a while, heroin ceased to be a fun experience. It wouldn't take "no" for an answer. We needed more to feel good—or feel anything at all— and the more we needed, the less we could afford. We may have resorted to stealing, cheating, or prostituting ourselves to get more heroin, though we wouldn't have called it that at the time. Many of us started using street heroin as our tolerance developed; we smoked, snorted, swallowed, and shot it.

For a long time, heroin was an effective pain reliever, but after a period of time we learned that no amount of the drug could numb our senses. No amount of the drug could keep real life from slipping in. Some of us began to use opiates to manage legitimate physical pain. Some of us found that opiates relieved us of the emotional pain that life had brought on. Over time, we all learned that we were experiencing intense spiritual pain and that heroin gave us a reprieve from this discomfort.

If you want to stop, there is a place for you in the rooms of Heroin Anonymous. We came here broken, full of self-hatred, alone, with legal problems, and afraid. Many of us had lost jobs, homes, and families. Many of us had already been to treatment and jail—often more than once. But we found a common solution for our addiction, and more importantly, we found each other. Together, we were able to escape heroin and start rebuilding our lives.

Today, we experience a sense of

peace and freedom that surpasses any high we felt when we were using. We found a way to live free of heroin, and so can you. If you want what we have—if you're really, truly *done*—Heroin Anonymous can help you stay clean. Using the spiritual tools we learned in HA and other Twelve Step programs, we never have to use again.

2

There is a Solution

When we were introduced to the Twelve Steps, we heard the word "surrender." This was the only thing we *hadn't* tried.

How do you surrender? We had struggled so long and so hard that we didn't know how to let go anymore. Heroin relaxed our painfully tight grip on reality – but how to do this without the drug?

The solution is based on a spiritual experience and involves embracing spiritual principles.

Through the Twelve Steps, we admit complete defeat and become honest, open-minded, and willing. Our sponsors guided us through the steps and helped us learn to trust in the solution. Our newfound freedom and the fellowship of HA have brought hope into an otherwise hopeless world. We were not consigned to imprisonment, death, or a life of using. *There is a solution.*

HA is a program based on simple spiritual principles. Through active work with others and a relationship with a power greater than yourself, you can learn to live without heroin, as many of us have in HA. The Steps have given us a life that was once a mere dream.

We have come to believe that there is a spiritual solution to our heroin problem. In order to get clean, we went to great lengths, trying every remedy we could think of. We went to treatment. We went to detox. We detoxed at home. We shot saline or tried weaning ourselves off. We switched to another substance, like cocaine or liquor. We deleted our dealers' numbers, only to get it again, or find a new connection. We moved. We swore that we really meant it this time. We went to jail, or prison.

At best, we lasted a few days. At worst, an hour, when the cravings asserted themselves. We tried and failed, tried and failed. We exhausted ourselves with failing. As Alcoholics Anonymous' book *The Twelve Steps and Twelve Traditions* says: "Our whole trouble had been the misuse of willpower. We had tried to bombard our problems with it instead of attempting to bring it into agreement with God's intention for us." As Heroin Anonymous members, we found this was true for us as well.

Today, our connections are no longer our drug dealers, the guy giving us cash for stolen goods, or doctors willing to prescribe to us. Our connections in HA are far different, but just as important. We connect to a Higher Power and our fellows in the program through service, meetings, and fellowship. We connect to ourselves through stepwork; in building a relationship with our sponsors, we find a new freedom as we build new lives for ourselves.

The same experience can be duplicated in 100 very different people, with the only necessary ingredients being honesty, openness, and willingness:

Honesty

This means telling the truth about who we are, what we've done, and what we hope for.

Openness

We have enough courage to connect with other people in recovery, plus enough desperation to throw our old ideas out the window. We have an open mind. We must, or the solution will not work for us.

Willingness

We are willing to try outside help, work with a sponsor, and change our ways for good. We may not always be willing. In this case, we pray for the willingness to become willing, and put ourselves in God's hands.

Starting with the small seed of surrender, we slowly developed spiritual roots. Once the heroin obsession was removed, we grew in miraculous, unexpected ways.

Our freedom comes from the Twelve Steps; our strength comes from the Higher Power; our hope comes from one another. We are no longer junkies, miserable and doomed. We have been recovered, and our solution will work for anyone willing to really try it.

3

An Honest Look

If you are here, you have experienced the unmanageability of life and the powerlessness of addiction. There is only one "must" in Heroin Anonymous. We had to admit we were sick people, and were powerless over heroin. For some, this was easy; others found it difficult. But we came to truly believe these things. We had to take of the filter and look at our lives honestly.

We often clung to the idea that somehow, some way, heroin would work for us. Hanging onto this idea is dangerous. We had to stop fighting. We had nothing left. There was no fight left in us. Asking for help and truly admitting that addiction had ruined us was our only option.

In other matters, we had amazing self-control, but heroin brought us to our knees. When we came to HA, we learned that powerlessness was actually an asset. Our greatest weakness became our greatest strength.

As we worked the Twelve Steps, it quickly became apparent that the faster we could let go of our self-will, the happier we would be. We had been taught to handle our problems on our own, but our addiction defeated us. We possessed no solutions capable of conquering this difficulty. Our ability to control some things gave us the wrong impression that we could manage all things. Pursuing this illusion shut us off from reality, other people, and God. In our addiction, it caused us to risk our lives and behave in a way we can only describe as insane.

Most of us were not aware that our problems ran much deeper than using heroin, but after a period of clean time, it was obvious that our problems came out of an inability to effectively cope with life. Luckily, our sponsors were aware of this and assured us that there was, in fact, a solution, and it all started with honesty. Having a clean date is a huge part of Step One. Our clean date is a strong sign that we were willing to look honestly at ourselves and our addiction.

This is not an easy thing to do. Pride and ego, especially in extreme cases like ours, will rarely allow us to admit defeat. We surrendered. We admitted we were powerless over heroin, and that our lives had become unmanageable. This is our first step.

In Step One, we gained an understanding of what insanity looked like in our lives. But now what? We were left with a very dark image, painted by our disease. We had to trust in a different solution, since our solution was killing us. We increased our chances of staying sober when we opened the door to the possibility of God. Why should we struggle?

We began to see that everything that had happened to us, good and bad, was not only meant to be but happened for a reason. Without our past, we would not be where we are today. Understanding this, our sanity began to return. When faced with decisions that used to baffle us, we were suddenly able to cope.

A sane person handles life on life's terms. Physical and mental health was restored. This often happened quickly, as we practiced a way of life that put our spiritual health first. Our instincts worked in our favor. We were increasingly able to do the next right thing. We had a solution. We were not alone. We came to believe that a Power greater than ourselves could restore us to sanity. This was our second step.

Letting go of our will and turning our lives over God is much like paddling a canoe against the current of a river. When we stop fighting the current and flow with the river, its power takes us where we need to go. We began Step Three when we made a decision to turn our will and life over to the care of God, as we understood God. How do we "turn over" these things?

Humility was something we might have experienced in small doses, or confused with humiliation. To fully invite God into our lives, we humbly accepted our finite selves. We admitted we needed divine help to recover. It really does take a miracle. When ready, we earnestly asked God to direct our lives. We asked God to accept us, to turn our mistakes and flaws into assets, and to demonstrate through us all that was possible. We asked God to use us as His tools, His agents.

When we did this, life became easier. Suddenly, we didn't have to do everything ourselves. We didn't have to win every argument, be first in line. We felt the subtle yet undeniable influence of our Creator, a gentle current guiding us.

As we worked Step Three, we learned to trust the Higher Power. We were not alone. We had entered a spiritual plane, and taken another step towards lifelong sobriety.

4

No More Secrets

As we enter into a relationship with our Creator through Steps One, Two, and Three, we begin to take down the high walls we built to keep the world away from us.

Heroin separated us from other humans, God, and ourselves. By working the Steps, we can reconnect. We discover that, in our innermost selves, is our link to the Divine. Our experience has shown that while these steps can be overwhelming and painful, we must not hesitate.

Honesty may be very difficult for a lot of us to define, as we had been living by a different moral code: the code dictated by the harsh realities of street life, hustling, and the buying and selling of heroin, ourselves, and other possessions. This way was in place long before our birth. For a long time, we were incapable of complete honesty. The lies and untruths allowed us to continue on in our addiction, and allowed us to survive our daily struggles. The process of deceiving others became a lifestyle and we found that even after we sobered up, the habit was hard to break.

But if we are going to recover, we need to practice rigorous honesty. We feel that this aspect of the program requires progress, not perfection. We suggest you start practicing honesty with one person: your sponsor. To work a proper Fourth Step, truly clean house, and experience some relief, we needed to be an open book.

Every member of our fellowship who has successfully stayed sober has completed this Step, thanks to God, a good sponsor, and enough desperation to be willing to break free from the heavy chains of the past. We must remember that honesty is an action, not a concept.

When we took an honest appraisal of our inventory, we could see that we weren't horrible people. We could begin to take responsibility for what we had done, and begin to forgive others for what they had done to us. We are not bad people trying to get good; we are sick people trying to get well, and our medicine is the Twelve Steps.

Imagine life with nothing to hide. No secrets, no lies, no dirty laundry. When we take Step Five with our sponsors, we admit to God, to ourselves, and to another human being the exact nature of our wrongs. We open ourselves up—not to criticism or condemnation, but to a new experience of relief and God's grace.

We have come to realize that discomfort is a positive feeling. When we feel discomfort, we are going beyond our old boundaries. We are trying something new, something different. This feeling seems most apparent in Step Four and Step Five. Our intuition tells us to stop when this feeling arises, to avoid the situation. But when we rely on our Higher Power and our sponsor, we realize this feeling is a green light. It's means it's time to *go*.

We cannot afford half measures in our personal recovery. We were not halfway junkies. We must commit wholeheartedly to this metamorphosis or risk failure, and for us failure is certain death.

We stopped performing for others, faking or playing in exchange for conditional acceptance. We stepped out of heroin's shadow and entered God's care. Once we started to comprehend our true selves—as God had made us, as our choices had shaped us, and as our experiences had influenced us—we were ready for the next Step.

During our inventory, we uncovered many of our defects of character. We began to see that heroin wasn't our problem; our problem was us. We were spiritually sick. We had a list of our defects, the warped places in our character that caused us to harm ourselves and others.

In Step Six, many of us are faced with a difficult situation. For as long as we could remember, these defects helped us walk through life. We fearlessly reviewed these deficiencies and took responsibility for our actions. Little did we know that these "shortcomings" were the cracks in our characters that would allow God to enter us, healing us and offering miraculous transformation.

We were grateful for our imperfections. We prayed for God's help, knowing His strength is perfect in our weakness.

We may look back at Step Three and gather the courage to press forward. We must become ready to leave these defects behind, as we learn a new way of life.

5

Why is 6 Afraid of 7?

Without some degree of humility, no heroin addict can stay sober. Unless more of this quality is developed than the bare minimum required for sobriety, we don't have much chance of becoming truly happy. Lack of humility is a sure sign of our spiritual sickness.

Remembering Step One—admitting our powerlessness over heroin addiction—we can see that we have already begun to practice humility. We have humbled ourselves in the face of an addiction that had taken over our lives. Formerly, we might have wallowed in self-pity and emotionalism, or avoided our defects entirely. If we are to stay sober, this is no longer an option. We take the bit in our teeth and offer our flawed, imperfect selves to our Maker. We trust that God doesn't make junk, and that with His help we can find the courage we need to grow into what He would have us be.

Step Eight seems simple enough. It is the planning period. By reviewing our inventory, we become aware of the people we harmed, and the way we warped our lives and our relationships. We caused physical, mental, emotional, financial, and spiritual harm.

As we wrote down the people and institutions we wronged, it was helpful to remember exactly what our part was in each situation. What had we done wrong? A good number of the people on our lists deserved amends of some sort. We owed them that much. But what about the ones that did not deserve our apologies? The ones we despised? The ones that had hurt us, as well?

We put aside our resentments and petty justifications and made a list of people we had harmed, *no matter what they had done to us*. Not forgetting to pray for guidance, we sought help from our sponsors. Becoming willing to make amends does not mean that we will confront each person on the list. The point is that we are willing to do anything and everything if it means we will stay sober. As we worked, whether we realized it or not, we were writing the road map for our escape. It is the way out of our old life, into the sunshine of the new.

As scary and painful as it may seem to make amends, the peace that waits for us on the other side of them is one of the greatest gifts we receive in recovery. Becoming fully aware of why we were making amends, and understanding the exact nature of our wrongs is absolutely crucial when taking our amends into action.

Making amends was not the same as saying "sorry." We had worn that word thin from overuse. We did not make amends to ease our guilt, win back family and friends, or puff up our already-bloated egos. We made amends to rectify the wrongs of the past. Remembering that through humility we gain strength, the amends we are about to make (however daunting they may seem) come as a welcome reprieve from the hell we had placed ourselves in. We did not shrink or make excuses this time. We determined how to make amends and went forward, always asking for God's help.

We said:

Creator, please give us patience and strength as we follow the path You have set before us. Help us to act with compassion and love. Please enter our hearts so we can do Your work well. We ask You to speak through us, giving us the right words for this task. Please help us to avoid conflict, resentment, and misunderstanding. We trust that our labor is acceptable to You. Amen.

6

Living the Program

The relief we felt from completing our amends was tremendous. We cleaned up the wreckage of the past. Now, from the other side, we experienced a new way of life which was truly miraculous. For the first time, the choked channel between us and our Creator was opened. Our perspective changed. We were made anew. We bring the vision of Steps One through Nine into our lives, learning how to live them instead of just doing them. We live the miracle when we live in the Steps.

Working the Tenth Step on a daily basis leads us to ask ourselves searching questions: Where was I wrong? Was I honest? What can I do to make things right? Was I of service? We handle wreckage in a much different way than we had in the past. We do not let our problems pile us. We nip resentments in the bud. We stop our selfish, hurtful behavior as quickly as it starts. We forgive in the same way we wish to be forgiven.

To take a daily inventory is more than looking at our defects, and what we did to harm others. It's important to look at our assets, what we've done throughout the day that we are proud of, as well. Things such as reaching out to another heroin addict, being of service, and simply showing up for our own recovery are all examples of estimable acts that build our character. The Tenth Step functions as a reinforcement of our daily reprieve.

The key to healing isn't locked in the addict's mind, though psychology and medicine may help with that aspect of the illness. The key is in his heart. Nobody knows what is written in your heart except you and your Creator. At the right time, you may be able to see this innermost part of yourself—which is pure, whole, and perfect—and wonder how the rest of you, and the world around you, got so fucked up. We use Steps Ten and Eleven to bring our inner and outer worlds into agreement.

We must never forget what brought us to this profoundly new place. We must never forget that it is God who is running our lives, not ourselves. Our newfound freedom and happiness are blessings bestowed by our Creator and his will for us.

Now, we had something to offer. We experienced serenity. We could stay sober in all conditions, even circumstances we formerly found unacceptable. Our willingness and desire to do this work produces the perennial fruit of recovery. The heart leads us to God—the heart speaks, and we listen. Each person's path to God is as individual as their experience, each as precious as the next. Having come this far, we trust that our Higher Power will continue to guide us as we grow.

7

A Spiritual Way

The Twelfth Step of Heroin Anonymous is: "Having had a spiritual awakening, we tried to carry the message to other heroin addicts, and to practice these principles in all our affairs." This miracle appeared when we applied ourselves to the previous eleven Steps; worked with a sponsor; regularly attended meetings; and helped other suffering addicts find a spiritual solution.

Through working the Twelve Steps, we slowly began to shed our old selves and our attachment to the past. We realized we had a new pair of glasses to view the world. Our reactions were different than they used to be. Our thinking had changed, and the new God-consciousness we cultivated in Step 11 permeated every aspect of our lives.

We were truly free, and we knew

that our sobriety was a debt we could never repay. To that end, we turned our lives over to God and did our best to perform His work in this brave new world. We worked with other heroin addicts. We shared our experience, strength, and hope, so that other people might have the same opportunity to get clean that we did. We knew that when we worked with another sick person, we had a better chance of keeping our sobriety. This work was all-important, and everything else was secondary to the service we gave to others.

We learned to be less selfish and give freely of what we had. We lost our fear of not having enough. Our faith increased, and with as it did, our hearts grew. We realized we had a special part to play in God's plan.

We continued to work Steps Ten, Eleven, and Twelve on a daily basis. Many of us, realizing that we were never going to be "cured" of addiction, repeated the Steps multiple times, each time gleaning more from the solution offered there.

We did these things, and so can you. We are free, through taking this simple program's suggestions and staying honest, open minded, and willing.

Although our own knowledge and experience is limited, we have shared what we believe to be true. More is revealed to all of us, daily, and we know God's plan is unfolding as it should. There is hope above all, and love, and miracles happening all around you. Seek them out. They are yours, if you want them.